NUMBER NINE

MEETING HOUSE ESSAYS

ANCIENT FONTS, MODERN LESSONS

T. Jerome Overbeck, SJ

MEETING HOUSE ESSAYS

ANCIENT FONTS, MODERN LESSONS

T. Jerome Overbeck, SJ

LTP

LITURGY
TRAINING
PUBLICATIONS

Special thanks to S. Anita Stauffer, my colleague in the North American Academy of Liturgy. Her assistance enabled me to formulate this sabbatical research project.

—T. Jerome Overbeck, SJ

Meeting House Essays was designed by Carolyn Riege, Kerry Perlmutter and Lisa Buckley, typeset in Goudy Old Style by James Mellody-Pizzato, and printed by Metro Litho in the United States of America. David Philippart was the editor, and Deborah Bogaert was the production editor. The photos on pages 3 and 15 are by Regina Kuehn; cover and other interior photos are by T. Jerome Overbeck, SJ.

Meeting House Essays is a series of papers reflecting on the mystery, beauty and practicalities of the place of worship, the house where the church meets God by meeting together.

Other Meeting House Essays

Number One: Sacred Places and the Pilgrimage of Life
               Lawrence Hoffman

Number Two: Acoustics for Liturgy
               A Collection of Articles of The Hymn Society in the United States
               and Canada

Number Three: Cherubim of Gold
               Building Materials and Aesthetics
               Peter E. Smith

Number Four: Places for Devotion
               John Buscemi

Number Five: Renewing the City of God
               The Reform of Catholic Architecture in the United States
               Michael E. DeSanctis

Number Six: Iconography and Liturgy
               Michael Jones-Frank

Number Seven: Lighting the Liturgy
               Viggo Bech Rambusch

Number Eight: Designing Future Worship Spaces
               The Mystery of a Common Vision
               Richard S. Vosko

ISBN 1-56854-091-4

Christian worship space is different from a theater, a class-room, a department store or a stadium. Any place designed specifically for Christian worship usually includes three key features that designate it as a Christian church. These features are: the altar (the table of the sacramental meal), the ambo or pulpit (the table of the word where the readings from the Bible are proclaimed and preached) and the baptismal font. This essay invites reflection on the baptismal font.

Think about the font in which you were baptized. Have baptismal fonts always looked this way? Why, until recently, did most baptismal fonts look this way? Your answers probably include functional considerations: You need a basin with a little bit of water over which parents hold their squirming infant while the priest or deacon drips water over the baby's forehead three times. That's correct: The design of the font is functional in the sense that it serves the rite of baptism as it is celebrated.

But an interesting thing about the design of the three essential furnishings in the Christian church building is this: Not only does form follow function, but form embodies meaning. Not only do we design baptismal fonts so that we can celebrate baptism, but also the way we celebrate baptism is largely determined by the design of the font. And all of this says something — literally, in stone — about what baptism means to Christians.

Examine the photographs on the next two pages. Do these early baptismal fonts resemble the one that you recalled from your own baptism or any of the fonts in church buildings where you have worshiped over the years?

This fourth-century font is in
Frejus, France.
Photo: T. Jerome Overbeck

This fifth-century font is in
Sbeitla, Tunisia.
Photo: T. Jerome Overbeck

This fifth-century font is in
Geneva, Switzerland.
Photo: T. Jerome Overbeck

These sixth-century fonts are currently in the Bardo Museum in Tunis, Tunisia.

Photos: T. Jerome Overbeck

This eighth-century font is in Aquilea, Italy, and is built on top of a fourth-century font.

Photo: T. Jerome Overbeck

Are there similarities between the fonts in these photographs and the fonts in the Christian churches you have known? Are there contrasts between these fonts and fonts that look more like wash basins, huge chalices or birdbaths? What difference does it make how a font is designed?

Many contemporary Christians fail to comprehend and appreciate what led early Christian communities to design these fonts the way they did. We assume too readily that we know what a baptismal font is supposed to look like.

In the fourth century and the subsequent early centuries, when Christianity became legal and popular, the church focused questions about baptism in a new way: by building fonts. Prior to this time, Christians usually were baptized—sometimes whole families at a time — by going to a nearby lake, stream or river. (Jesus was baptized in the Jordan River.) But with the increased numbers of people preparing for baptism (called *catechumens*), places designed specifically for baptism became necessary.

These early Christian communities asked themselves questions about how best to communicate and to cultivate the faith-filled meanings of baptism. In response, they chose the nakedness of those to be baptized and the use of large amounts of water as the two primary symbols by which to ritually enact and deepen the radical meanings of incorporating in themselves Jesus' dying and being born into resurrected life. Due to these considerations, the adult-size font became the norm.

Having to design baptismal fonts was a new situation for early Christians. They asked the overarching questions—What does it mean to be baptized? How do we celebrate baptism?— and these questions led to practical questions about the shape, location, size, depth and accessibility of the font. (In some places, the font was in a building separate from the main hall in which the church worshiped. It was open only for baptism and only to the baptized ministers and those who were to be baptized at that moment. The sacredness of baptism — as well as the need for at least some privacy for the naked candidates — was embodied by controlled access to the font.)

Today we need to learn again how to ask these questions. It would serve us well not to jump to practical answers without sufficiently pondering the fundamental questions that lie beneath them. Otherwise, without realizing it and with the best of intentions, we can mistakenly fall into the path of least resistance, into commonly accepted ways of proceeding without adequate regard for a fuller understanding. Instead, we need to make informed decisions, decisions that are made in light of history, theology and the best current pastoral perspectives available.

Contemporary Christians can easily get caught in a "designer mentality," proceeding with their concerns focused primarily or merely on color coordination, ambiance and other fashionable trends. Unfortunately, much recent baptismal practice has been preoccupied with the superficial in other ways as well.

For example, it is discouraging when the questions of ultimate significance become: Do we have to have a swimming pool in our new church? Is there a way to do this baptism without messing up my hair? Also, the meaning behind the choice of godparents can get reduced to a "return favor" (you asked me so now I'll ask you), a family perk, a tactic to garner favor within one's family or circle of friends, or even as a business strategy. But none of these attitudes will help us encounter the mystery at the heart of baptism; indeed, they will hinder us from participating in it. Instead, we must search out ways of entering into the rites of baptism authentically and fully. And there is no better way to begin than by asking the questions that earlier churches grappled with and discerning their answers as they designed fonts and celebrated baptism.

In light of the recent recovery of early church tradition, the current liturgical reform encourages a fuller use of primary symbols, such as water, oil, bread and wine, and so on. Baptizing by immersion ritualizes the fact that Christian living is messy and deals with realities more far-reaching than the superficial. Through word and gesture, we attempt to give flesh and blood to the fundamental, radical meanings associated with baptism by the lavish use of water. ("Immersion" does not necessarily mean "submersion." You can see from the photos that some of these ancient fonts are not large or deep enough for putting an adult completely underwater. Immersion most commonly means that a person stands or kneels in a good amount of water while more water is poured copiously over his or her head.)

Early church leaders articulated some of these deeper meanings as they reflected with the newly baptized upon their experience of baptism by immersion. In the mid-fourth century, to help those recently baptized understand more about their baptism, Cyril of Jerusalem wrote:

> After that you were led to the holy font of divine baptism, as Christ was brought from the cross to the tomb which is before our eyes. And each of you was asked if he believed in the name of the Father and of the Son and of the Holy Spirit. And you made the saving confession, and descended three times into the water and came up again, here also recalling by a symbol the

three-day burial of Christ. For as our Savior passed three days and three nights in the tomb of the earth, so you also in your first ascent out of the water initiated the first day of Christ in the earth, and by your descent, the night. As he who is in the night no longer sees, but he who is in the day remains in the light, so in the descent as in the night, you saw nothing, but in ascending again, you were in the day.[1]

Toward the end of the fourth century, Gregory of Nyssa described how the ritual of baptism represents burial and rising to new life:

> And when we receive baptism, in imitation of our Lord and Master and Guide, we are not buried in the earth (for this is cover for the body that is completely dead, enveloping as it does the weakness and corruption of our nature), but we come to the element kindred to the earth, water, and conceal ourselves in it as the Savior did in the earth; and doing this three times we picture to ourselves, the third-day grace of the resurrection.[2]

Leo the Great in Rome drew upon the analogy between the womb of Jesus' mother and the baptismal water of a Christian:

> It is his spiritual birth that each one acquires in regeneration. To everyone that is reborn, the water of baptism is like the Virgin, so that the sin which was nullified there by that sacred conception may be removed here by the mystic washing.[3]

Baptism is a time of ritual bathing, a washing that has mystic significance. The fonts of early churches embodied an understanding that individuals of the family were being bathed. A small basin on a pedestal is hardly equivalent to a bathtub.

In the recent past, we may have been overly concerned with questions about efficiency and pragmatism. This led to minimalism in terms of the signs of the sacraments. For example, one question was, How much water needs to be poured to still have the baptism work? But this is not the most important question. As a sacrament, as a liturgy, baptism is one of the most significant and foundational ways that Christians worship God together. Sacraments and liturgy "work" by way of signs, signs that are perceptible to the senses. "You give us grace through sacramental signs," we say to God in the prayer to bless the water for baptism. So we can afford a little more care in focusing upon the font as a place for burial, birth and bath.[4]

8

This hexagonal font recalls the sixth day, Friday, the day of Christ's passion into which we are baptized.

Photo: T. Jerome Overbeck

The sixth- or seventh-century hexagonal font pictured above (Servus), in Sbeitla, Tunisia, not only enabled both adults and children to be immersed individually into the depths of the baptismal waters but also emphasized the meaning of dying with Jesus. One plunges into a six-sided font and is invited to remember the sixth day of the week, Friday, the day of Christ's crucifixion: "Remember the one Friday we call good because Jesus cared enough about people to remain faithful in his love, even when it meant dying."

This kind of "remembering" that Christians do (in Greek, *anamnesis*) is similar to the "remembering" of the Hebrew tradition in biblical times. It brings the past into the present and starts the future in the present. Christians recall Jesus' death at a specific place and time in the past, how these tragic events happened and all they meant in faith for the world. Christians also remember the dying of Jesus present in the self-sacrifice required of them and others now as they choose to follow Jesus in the circumstances of their lives. Christians also remember their commitment to the baptismal belief that the only way to go into the future is by living here and then forever in Jesus' pattern: "Dying you destroyed our death, rising you restored our life. Lord Jesus, come in glory!"

The font pictured on the next page, a fourth-century octagonal font in Milan, enabled adults to be immersed.[5] But why is the font octagonal? coincidence? the designer's whim? This choice hints at the meaning of life in Christ as understood by the people who designed, built and baptized in this font. Since

This octagonal font recalls the "eighth day," or eternity. Baptism leads to eternal life.
Photo: T. Jerome Overbeck

there are seven days in the week, eternity was often envisioned as the "eighth day." Sunday, as the Day of the Lord, was seen to be a sign of the eighth day. Baptism was often celebrated on Sunday — and especially at Easter — because by baptism we are heirs to eternity, children of the eighth day. The octagonal shape emphasizes the meaning of rising to eternal life. One plunges into an eight-sided font and is invited to remember the eighth day of the week.

If we think as the world does, there are only seven days in a week. But as Christians, we put on the mind of Christ and think differently than other people do in some fundamental respects. We believe that we can rise above self-absorption through dying to self. We believe that we can find life through the countless forms of death in the human sojourn. Suffering and death do not have the final word in the book of life. This is at the heart of the mystery that we encounter in the celebration of baptism. This is what the design of the baptismal font must somehow evoke.

Look at the eighth-century octagonal font on the next page, found in Cividale, Italy. There were steps going up to this font, on one side, and the person to be baptized actually climbed into the font, which resembles a luxurious bath. We tend to bathe or shower more frequently today and so take it for granted. But even today, we bathe babies after they emerge from the womb and bathe the bodies of the dead in preparation for the funeral. In some parts of the ancient world, bathing before one's wedding was an important preparation, not only to get clean physically but to prepare spiritually for marriage. All of these bathing associations are evoked by this eighth-century font from Italy — a country famous for its public baths.

Christ enables us, "time after time," to break through old habits to a new kind of living, to gain a "fresh, clean start."

The interior of this font (pictured below) is reminiscent of a public bath. But here, the washing is mystical as well as physical.

Photo: T. Jerome Overbeck

The intricately carved exterior evokes a luxurious bath.

Photo: T. Jerome Overbeck

Forgiving, faithful love washes over us, creating new possibilities precisely when the short-sighted, doubting parts of ourselves can mire us in dead-end alternatives. As Christ died and then rose from the dead, for each of us Christians new life is drawn out of, borne out of, the many deaths that we undergo.

11

This third-century font from Dura-Europas evokes both the bath and the tomb.

Photo: T. Jerome Overbeck

The image of baptism as dying to self is further linked to the passion of Christ when the font is cruciform.

Photo: T. Jerome Overbeck

The third-century font at the top of this page is at Dura-Europas, and it likewise picks up on the bathing imagery but develops it in another, surprising direction. In its culture, this font resembled a tomb: The bath from which the new person was born was a sarcophagus in which the old self was buried. The sixth-century font pictured underneath it, which is in Israel, evokes the same mystery and explicitly identifies it with

This womb-shaped font, with steps for descending into the waters and steps for ascending from them, evokes images of birth and life-as-process.

Photo: T. Jerome Overbeck

Christ: The font is shaped like Christ's cross, and the one to be baptized literally descends into the cross and rises from it. Both these fonts heightened people's awareness of plunging into Jesus' pattern of dying as the only way to life that lasts. They also emphasized to those who built and used them that life is a process of putting on this pattern. Baptismal life is a recurring movement: Notice the steps in the cruciform font.

Some new fonts today have two sets of steps: one set by which the person enters the font and another (sometimes oriented toward the altar) by which the person exits. Passing through a font in this way ritualizes life as a process. Baptism makes present Jesus' definitive, once-and-for-all, unconditionally embracing love of the forgiving God. It also ritualizes the fact that often we must pass through many death-dealing circumstances yet believe that we will emerge victorious with Jesus in the end. The Christian remains hopeful in the process because of faith. In faith the believer knows and celebrates that God's ways of saving in Jesus take time and are not magical and instantaneous. (That's why we renew our baptismal vows every year at Easter.)

Toward the end of the fourth century in Milan, Ambrose preached about the meaning of the baptismal rite:

> Yesterday we discussed the font, which shows, as it were, the form of the tomb, which we enter as we profess our faith in the Father and the Son and the Holy Spirit, and in which we are dipped under and come up, that is, rise again.[6]

The fifth-century, womb-shaped font (Vitalis) pictured above, in Sbeitla, Tunisia (figure 6), enabled adults to be immersed individually and emphasized the meaning of being born again.

One plunged into this font, passing through it as if through a birth canal, and emerged a new-born Christian. In Rome, nearly 100 years before this was built, Leo the Great reflected upon the birth of new life:

> There (in the mystery of regeneration) the earth of sin is the life of the reborn, and the Lord's three-day death is reproduced by the threefold immersion (*triduanam Domini mortem imitatur trina demersio*). By the removal, as it were, of the stone before the sepulchre, those who enter the womb of the font and are old are given birth by the water of baptism and become new.[7]

Augustine used some of this same natal imagery when preaching about baptism: "The mother's womb was the water of baptism."[8]

Earlier in this essay it was stated that ancient churches employed two fundamental signs in celebrating baptism: the nakedness of those being baptized and lavish use of water. Both attest to the mystery of birth (we are born naked), bathing (we bathe naked) and death (even though we may be buried clothed, we take no material with us — we leave this world, metaphorically, as naked as we came into it). Given present sensibilities, employing nakedness as a primary vehicle for communicating and cultivating primal baptismal meanings seems out of the question. However, recovering the more traditional use of immersing as the primary ritual gesture seems timely.

During the 1994 international conference of Societas Liturgica in Fribourg, Switzerland, ecumenical Christian scholars frequently acknowledged the value of recovering adult immersion as the norm for the designing and constructing of Christian baptismal fonts. Parishes that use such fonts already experience the visceral responses not only of the ones being baptized but also of the entire assembly. For example, during the immersion of adults at the Easter Vigil at Loyola University, Chicago, invariably when the videotape is replayed months after the ceremony for teaching purposes,[9] there are observable, audible interactions with those being baptized and with others in the assembly.

At the liturgy, worshipers maneuver to see better, to participate by attending to the action. Some get up and walk closer to the event. Many express in some fashion their own inner movements through guttural sounds. In talking with people in the assembly afterward, it is clear that more than a "greeting card" approach to baptism is occurring. This is more than a calculated warm fuzzy, the manipulation of something of major significance through faddish form; for the impact of such a trendy

approach is short-lived. Not so with immersion at the Vigil. Months after the fact, those who worshiped at Loyola's Vigil still reflect upon the continuing meaning of baptism for them in their own interior lives. They themselves were engaged in the ritual action[10] with full, conscious and active participation — the goal of Christian liturgy.[11]

Baptism is messy and evokes meanings over which no one has easy control. Christians need to embody this more clearly. Literally building in the capability of immersion by providing an appropriate font enables the church to recover the more traditional ways of baptizing and the many primal understandings associated with such a profound ritual.

NOTES

1. Cyril of Jerusalem, *Catechesis Mystigogicae* 2:4 (Florilegium Patristicum 7:83, by Quasten).

2. Gregory of Nyssa, *In baptismum Christi* (Patrologicae Graeca 46:585, by J.P. Migne).

3. Leo the Great, *Sermones 24, In nativitate Domini* (Patrilogian Latina 54:206, by J.P. Migne).

4. S. Anita Stauffer, "The Font as Symbol: A Place for Burial, Birth and Bath," *Liturgy*, vol. 5, no. 4 (spring 1986).

5. This is the font in which Bishop Ambrose baptized Augustine as an adult at the Easter Vigil in 387. The circumference of this font is more than 19 meters, and its depth is about one meter.

6. Ambrose, *De Sacramentis* 3:1:1 (Florilegium Patristicum 7:151, by Quasten).

7. Leo the Great, *Sermones 70, De passione Domini* (Patrilogia Latina 54:382, by J.P. Migne).

8. Augustine, *Sermones 119* (Patrologia Latina 38:364, by J.P. Migne).

9. "Easter Vigil 1995," Chicago: Loyola University Center for Instructional Design, 1995. See also Liturgy Training Publications' video *This Is the Night*, which shows the celebration of the Vigil (with immersion baptism) at St. Pius V Church in Pasadena, Texas.

10. As was true in the classical baptismal liturgy in Rome, the role of the assembly was anything but to be passive spectators. See foreword by Mark Searle in Regina Kuehn, *A Place for Baptism* (Chicago: Liturgy Training Publications, 1992).

11. *Constitution on the Sacred Liturgy*, 14.

FOR FURTHER REFLECTION

From this noble spring a saving water gushes which cleanses all human defilement. Do you wish to know the benefits of the sacred water? These streams give the faith that regenerates. Wash away the defilement of your past life in the sacred fountain.

Surpassing joy to share in the life the water brings! Whoever resorts to this spring abandons earthly things and tramples underfoot the works of darkness.

Baptistry inscription, date unknown
St. Lawrence in Damaso

The brood born here to live in heaven has life from water and the fructifying Spirit. Sinner, seek your cleansing in this stream that takes the old and gives a new person back. No barrier can divide where life unites: One faith, one fount, one Spirit make one people. A virgin still, the church gives birth to children conceived of God, delivered in the water. Washed in this bath the stains will float away that mark the guilt of Adam and your own. The stream that flows below sprang from the wounded Christ to wash the whole world clean and give it life. Children of the water, think no more of earth; heaven will give you joy; in heaven hope. Think not your sins too many or too great: Birth in this stream is birth to holiness.

Baptistry inscription, fifth century
St. John Lateran, Rome

In the liturgy, by means of signs perceptible to the senses, human sanctification is signified and brought about in ways proper to each of these signs.

Constitution on the Sacred Liturgy, 7

Baptism by immersion is the fuller and more expressive sign of the sacrament and, therefore, provision should be made for its more frequent use in the baptism of adults. The provision of the *Rite of Christian Initiation of Adults* for partial immersion, namely, immersion of the candidate's head, should be taken into account.

National Statutes for the Catechumenate, 17
United States Bishops

To speak of symbols and of sacramental signification is to indicate that immersion is the fuller and more appropriate symbolic action in baptism [Rite of Baptism for Children (BC), introduction]. New baptismal fonts, therefore, should be constructed to allow for the immersion of infants, at least, and to allow for the pouring of water over the entire body of a child or adult. Where fonts are not so constructed, the use of a portable one is recommended.

The place of the font, whether it is an area near the main entrance of the liturgical space or one in the midst of the congregation, should facilitate full congregational participation, regularly in the Easter Vigil [Ibid. no. 25]. If the baptismal space is in a gathering place or entry way, it can have living, moving water, and include provision for warming the water for immersion.

Environment & Art in Catholic Worship, 76 – 77
U.S. Bishops' Committee on the Liturgy

17.1 The baptistry is the area which contains the baptismal font, or in which the baptismal water flows. The area should be reserved for the celebration of baptism and should be located and designed with the utmost care.

17.2 Baptism is the first of three sacraments by which a person is initiated into the people of God, the Church. It is "the door to life and to the kingdom of God" (General Introduction, *Christian Initiation,* 3)

(In confirmation the baptized continue on their path of initiation, are enriched with the gift of the Spirit and are more closely linked with the Church. Finally, the baptized come to the table of the eucharist to join Christ in offering his sacrifice and to receive his body and blood in communion.)

17.3 The meaning and effects of baptism are expressed in its celebration through powerful images, mostly of a biblical nature: passage from darkness to light, from slavery to freedom, from blindness to vision, from death to life; dying and rising with Christ expressed through immersion in and emergence from water as from a tomb; washing and purification; destruction of the old within us, and rebirth; the stripping off of the old and the clothing in the new; creation and re-creation; singing and anointings, vitality and growth.

17.7 The design of the place for each stage of the celebration of the sacrament requires consideration of the activities which occur at each place and of the relationship between them.

17.8 With the exception of the sanctuary and the space in which the Blessed Sacrament is reserved no area in the church is excluded as a possible location for the baptistry, provided the area is large enough to accommodate a good number of people, and provided the faithful can participate in the celebration of the sacrament.

In this connection it may be noted that the entrance has a particular significance in relation to baptism, the first step in our "entrance" or initiation into the people of God. Here the baptism of children or the admission of catechumens normally begins.

It should be remembered that the ideal occasion for the celebration is the Paschal Vigil, that the celebration may take place occasionally at Sunday Mass, and that at other times too a large number of the faithful may be present. The location of the baptistry should facilitate the participation of the faithful on these occasions.

17.9 The baptismal area should be large enough to accommodate with ease the priest or deacon, the candidates, families, godparents, ministers and others who may be involved. The liturgy envisages the presence of "the people of God, represented not only by the parents, godparents and relatives, but also as far as possible by friends, neighbors and some members of the local church"(GICI, 7).

17.10 There is to be a baptistry with a baptismal font in all parish churches. Other churches or oratories will have these only if they have acquired the right already, or with the approval of the local Ordinary (Code of Canon Law, 858).

17.12 The font should be designed in such a way that it is suitable for the baptism of adults as well as infants. It should be able to accommodate adults for baptism by immersion — at least by partial immersion. Even when it is not being used, the baptismal font should express something of the dignity and mystery of the sacrament. . . .

Because of the possibility of immersion, consideration should be given to the provision of facilities for drying and dressing.

17.13 The font may take any of several different forms (with, e.g., moving, "living" water) and draw inspiration in its design from the rich symbolism associated with the waters of baptism.

If it can be done without obscuring the view of the font by those present at a baptism, a step or steps down to and up from the font may be provided as a means of expressing burial and resurrection with Christ.

The Place of Worship
Irish Episcopal Commission for Liturgy

ORDER FOR THE BLESSING OF A BAPTISTRY OR OF A NEW BAPTISMAL FONT

from the BOOK OF BLESSINGS

INTRODUCTION

1080 The baptistry or site of the baptismal font is rightly considered to be one of the most important parts of a church. For it is the place for celebrating baptism, the first sacrament of the New Law, through which those who firmly accept Christ in faith and receive the Spirit of adoption[1] become in name and in fact God's adopted children.[2] Joined with Christ in a death and resurrection like his,[3] they become part of his Body.[4] Filled with the anointing of the Spirit, they become God's holy temple[5] and members of the Church, "a chosen race, a royal priesthood, a holy nation, God's own people."[6]

1081 Because baptism is the beginning of the entire Christian life, every cathedral and parish church ought to have its own baptistry or a special place where the baptismal font flows or is situated. For pastoral reasons and with the consent of the local Ordinary,[7] other churches or chapels may have a baptistry or baptismal font.

1082 In the building of a baptistry or in the setting up of a baptismal font the primary consideration must be the proper and worthy celebration of the rites of baptism, as these are set out in the *Rite of Baptism for Children* and in the *Rite of Christian Initiation of Adults*.

1083 In the case both of a baptistry that is erected apart from the main body of the church for the celebration of the entire baptismal rite and of a font that is set up within the church itself, everything must be arranged in such a way as to bring out the connection of baptism with the word of God and with the eucharist, the high point of Christian initiation.

1084 A baptistry separated from the body of the church is to be worthy of the sacrament celebrated there and is to be set aside exclusively for baptism,[8] as befits the place where, from the womb of the Church, so to speak, Christians are reborn through water and the Holy Spirit.

1085 The baptismal font, particularly one in a baptistry, should be stationary, gracefully constructed out of a suitable material, of splendid beauty and spotless cleanliness; it should permit baptism by immersion, wherever this is the usage.[9] In order to enhance its force as a sign, the font should be designed in such a way that it functions as a fountain of running water; where the climate requires, provision should be made for heating the water.[10]

RITE OF BLESSING

1086 When a new baptistry has been erected or a new font installed, it is opportune to celebrate a special rite of blessing. But in the case simply of a portable vessel "in which on occasion the water is prepared for celebration of the sacrament in the sanctuary," this special rite is not celebrated.[11]

MINISTER OF THE RITE

1087 The reception of baptism stands as the beginning of the faithful's life in Christ that in some way derives from and depends on their high priest, the bishop.[12] In his own diocese the bishop himself, then, should dedicate a new baptistry or new baptismal font. But he may entrust this duty to another bishop or a priest, especially to one who is his associate and assistant in the pastoral care of the faithful for whom the new baptistry or font is intended. When a bishop is the celebrant, everything in the rite should be adapted accordingly.

CHOICE OF DAY

1088 As a rule the day designated for the celebration of the blessing should be a Sunday, especially a Sunday of the Easter season or the Sunday or feast of the Baptism of the Lord, in order to bring out more clearly the paschal character of baptism and to make possible a large attendance of the faithful.

The rite of blessing may not be celebrated on Ash Wednesday, during Holy Week, or on All Souls Day.

PASTORAL PREPARATION

1089 The erection of a new baptistry or baptismal font is an important event in the life of a Christian community. The celebration of the blessing should therefore be announced to the faithful well ahead of time and they should be properly prepared to take an active part in the rite. They should be particularly well instructed about the significance of the baptismal font and its sign value, so that they will be inspired with a renewed reverence and appreciation toward baptism and toward the font as a symbol of baptism.

REQUISITES

1090 The following are to be prepared for the rite of blessing a baptistry or a new baptismal font:

- the font filled with water;
- the Easter candle for the procession;
- candlestand for the Easter candle;
- Roman Ritual;
- Lectionary for Mass;
- censer and boat containing incense;
- container to receive the newly blessed water and sprinkler;
- chairs for the celebrant and other ministers.

When baptism is to be celebrated, all the requisites for celebrating the sacrament are also to be made ready.

1091 The color of the vestments for the rite is white or another festive color. The following are to be prepared:

- for a bishop: alb, pectoral cross, stole, cope or, if he is to celebrate Mass, chasuble, miter, and pastoral staff;
- for priests: alb and stole, or Mass vestments;
- for deacons: alb, stole (dalmatic);
- for other ministers: alb or other lawfully approved liturgical vesture.

ORDER OF BLESSING OF A NEW BAPTISMAL FONT WITHOUT THE CELEBRATION OF BAPTISM

INTRODUCTORY RITES

1109 In the way indicated in no. 1092, when the community has gathered, the celebrant and ministers proceed from the sacristy through the body of the church to the baptistry.

[1092 When the community has gathered, the celebrant, priests, deacons, and ministers, all with their proper vestments, proceed from the sacristy through the body of the church to the baptistry; they are led by a censer bearer carrying a censer with lighted charcoal; they are followed by an acolyte bearing the Easter candle and by other persons in the procession.]

1110 During the procession one of the following antiphons with Psalm 36 and the doxology is sung, or some other suitable song.

Antiphon: You will drink of the Lord's waters of delight, of the fountains of salvation.

Or:

Antiphon: Lord, you are the source of life, and in the light of your glory we see light.

PSALM 36

O LORD, your kindness reaches to heaven,
your faithfulness, to the clouds.
Your justice is like the mountains of God;
your judgments, like the mighty deep;
man and beast you save, O LORD. *R.*

How precious is your kindness, O God!
The children of men take refuge in the shadow of your wings.
They have their fill of the prime gifts of your house;
from your delightful stream you give them to drink. *R.*

For with you is the fountain of life,
and in your light we see light.
Keep up your kindness toward your friends,
your just defense of the upright of heart. *R.*

Glory to the Father, and to the Son, and to the Holy Spirit:
as it was in the beginning, is now, and will be for ever.
Amen. *R.*

1111 When the procession reaches the baptistry, all go and stand in their assigned places. The Easter candle is placed on the candlestand prepared for it at the center of the baptistry or near the font. When the singing has ended, the celebrant greets those present in the following or other suitable words, taken mainly from sacred Scripture.

The grace of our Lord Jesus Christ and the love of God and the fellowship of the Holy Spirit be with you all.

All make the following or some other suitable reply:

And also with you.

1112 In the following or similar words, the celebrant prepares those present for the blessing.

My dear brothers and sisters, we have come together to carry out a joyous celebration. We are about to bless a new baptismal font for all who will come forth reborn from it. Receiving God's mercy, they will, as a result of their baptism, become members of a people set apart, the Church; they will be joined to Christ, the firstborn of many brothers and sisters, and, having received the Holy Spirit of adoption, they will dare to call upon God as Father in virtue of being his children.

1113 After his introductory remarks, the celebrant, with hands joined, says:

Let us pray.

All pray briefly in silence; then, with hands outstretched, the celebrant continues:

O God,
by the sacrament of rebirth
you continually increase the number of your children.
Grant that all who will come forth
    reborn from this saving font
may by their way of life give glory to your name
and add to the holiness of the Church, their mother.

We ask this through Christ our Lord.

Response: Amen.

READING OF THE WORD OF GOD

1114 After the introductory rites, the celebrant sits. Then one or more texts of sacred Scripture are read, taken from those provided in the Lectionary for Mass for use in the celebration of Christian initiation apart from the Easter Vigil[14] or for us in the celebration of baptism of children.[15] Between the readings there is a responsorial psalm, related to the reading that preceded it, or an interval of silence. The gospel reading always holds the place of honor.

1115 After the reading of the word of God, the celebrant in the homily explains the biblical texts, so that those present may better understand the importance of baptism and the symbolism of the font.

BLESSING OF THE NEW FONT

1116 In the following or similar words, the celebrant invites the faithful to prayer.

My dear brothers and sisters, the time has come to bless this font through the prayer of the Church, that the gift of the Holy Spirit will endow its waters with the power to sanctify. But we should first pray to God our Father that he will keep the faith alive in our community and increase the bonds of love between us. For the font of baptism is truly opened when our ears are heedful of God's word; when our minds are brightened with Christ's light and closed to the darkness of sin; when our hearts are bound closely to the Lord and renounce Satan and all his works.

1117 All pray briefly in silence; then, turning to the font, the celebrant, with hands outstretched, says:

Lord God,
Creator of the world
and Father of all who are born into it,
it is right that we should give you praise
for allowing us to open this saving font
through the liturgy of your Church.

Here the door is reopened to the life of the spirit
and the gateway to the Church is swung wide
to those against whom the gates of paradise were shut.
This pool is opened and in it the newness of its pure waters
will again make clean and spotless
those who were stained by the old ways of sin.
A new torrent is released
whose gushing waters sweep away sin
and bring new virtue to life.
A stream of living water, coming from Christ's side, now flows
and those who drink this water will be brought to eternal life.
Over this font the lamp of faith spreads the holy light
that banishes darkness from the mind
and fills those who are reborn here with heavenly gifts.
Those who profess their faith at this font
are plunged beneath the waters and joined to Christ's death,
so that they may rise with him to newness of life.

Lord,
we ask you to send the life-giving presence of your Spirit
    upon this font,
placed here as the source of new life for your people.
The power of the Spirit made the Virgin Mary the mother
    of your Son;
send forth the power of the same Spirit,
so that your Church may present you
with countless new sons and daughters
and bring forth new citizens of heaven.

Grant, O Lord, that the people who are reborn from this font
may fulfill in their actions
what they pledge by their faith
and show by their lives
what they begin by the power of your grace.
Let the people of different nations and conditions
who come forth as one from these waters of rebirth
show by their love that they are brothers and sisters
and by their concord that they are citizens
    of the one kingdom.
Make them into true sons and daughters
who reflect their Father's goodness,
disciples who are faithful to the teaching of their one Master,
temples in whom the voice of the Spirit resounds.
Grant that they may be witnesses to the Gospel,
doers of the works of holiness.
Enable them to fill with the Spirit of Christ

the earthly city where they live,
until they are welcomed home in the heavenly Jerusalem.
We ask this through Christ our Lord.

Response: Amen.

1118 After the invocation over the font, the celebrant places incense in the censer and incenses the font; during this time, a baptismal song may be sung, for example, one of the following antiphons.

Antiphon: The Lord's voice resounding over the waters, the Lord over the vastness of the waters.

Or:

Antiphon: The Father's voice calls us above the waters, the glory of the Son shines on us, the love of the Spirit fill us with life.

Or:

Antiphon: This is the fountain of life, the water made holy by the suffering of Christ, washing all the world.

1119 As circumstances suggest, when the baptismal song is over, all may renew their profession of baptismal faith. The celebrant address the faithful in these or similar words.

Brothers and sisters, call to mind at this moment the faith you professed when you received the sacraments of Christian initiation, so that, led by the grace of the Holy Spirit, you may have the power to live up to it more fully each day.

The celebrant then asks all present:

Do you believe in God, the Father almighty,
    creator of heaven and earth?

All:

I do.

Celebrant:

Do you believe in Jesus Christ, his only Son, our Lord,
    who was born of the Virgin Mary,
    was crucified, died, and was buried,
    rose from the dead,
    and is now seated at the right hand of the Father?

All:

I do.

Celebrant:

Do you believe in the Holy Spirit,
the holy Catholic Church, the communion of saints,
the forgiveness of sins, the resurrection of the body,
and the life everlasting?

All:

I do.

The celebrant expresses his own assent to the profession of faith by proclaiming the faith of the Church in the following formulary. But, as occasion suggests, another formulary may be substituted or a song that allows all in the assembly to proclaim their faith together.

This is our faith. This is the faith of the church.
We are proud to profess it in Christ Jesus our Lord.

Response: Amen.

1120 then the celebrant takes the sprinkler and sprinkles the assembly with water from the newly blessed font, as all sing an antiphon, for example:

Antiphon: I saw water flowing from the right side of the temple, alleluia. It brought God's life and his salvation, and the people sang in joyful praise: alleluia, alleluia.
(See Ezekiel 47:1 – 2)

Or:

Antiphon: I will pour clean water over you and wash away all your defilement.

CONCLUDING RITE

1121 As circumstances suggest, the intercessions may be said. The celebrant introduces them and an assisting minister or one of those present announces the intentions. From the following intentions those best suited to the occasion may be used or adapted, or other intentions that apply to the particular circumstances may be composed.

The celebrant says:

Through the paschal mystery our loving Father has given us rebirth from water and the Holy Spirit into a new life as his own children. With hearts united let us pray to him, saying:

Response: Lord, renew in us the wonders of your power.

Or:

Response: Lord, hear our prayer.

Assisting minister:

Father of mercies, you have created us in your own image and sanctified us through baptism; make us always and everywhere conscious of your gift and of our Christian dignity. (For this we pray:) *R.*

Assisting minister:

From the side of Christ you brought forth the waters of the Holy Spirit; make this life-giving water that we receive become for us a fountain of living water leaping up to provide eternal life. (For this we pray:) *R.*

Assisting minister:

In the waters of baptism you have made us a chosen race, a royal priesthood, a holy people; grant that we will fulfill our Christian responsibilities by proclaiming your goodness to all. (For this we pray:) *R.*

Assisting minister:

You constantly increase your Church with new members; grant that all those reborn in the water of this font will live up to what they have acknowledged in faith. (For this we pray:) *R.*

Assisting minister:

In your kindness you have permitted us to erect this new baptismal font; grant that for catechumens it will become the pool of new life and for all of us a reminder of constant renewal of life. (For this we pray:) *R.*

1122 The celebrant then introduces the Lord's Prayer in these or similar words.

Remembering that our baptism gave us the spirit of adopted children and mindful of our Savior's command, let us pray to our heavenly Father, saying:

All:

Our Father . . .

The celebrant continues immediately:

O God,
who endowed these waters with the power of death and life,
grant that those who are buried with Christ in this font
may put aside all sin

and rise again with him,
clothed in the radiant garment of immortality.

We ask this through Christ our Lord.

Response: Amen.

1123 After the blessing, a song expressing paschal joy and thanks-giving or the Canticle of Mary may be sung.

1124 The assisting deacon then dismisses the people in the usual way.

NOTES

1. See Romans 8:15.

2. See 1 John 3:1; John 1:12; Romans 9:8.

3. See Romans 6:5.

4. See Ephesians 5:30; 1 Corinthians 12:27; Romans 12:5.

5. See 1 Corinthians 3:16 – 17 and 6:19; 2 Corinthians 6:16; Ephesians 2:21 – 22.

6. 1 Peter 2:9.

7. See Roman Ritual, *Rite of Baptism for Children*, Introduction, no. 11.

8. Roman Ritual, *Rite of Baptism for Children:* Christian Initiation, General Introduction, no. 25.

9. See ibid., no. 22.

10. Ibid., no. 20.

11. Ibid., no. 19.

12. See SC, art. 41.

14. See Lectionary for Mass (2nd ed., 1981), nos. 751 – 755 (Ritual Masses, I. Christian Initiation, 1. Order of Catechumens and Christian Initiation of Adults, Celebration of the Sacraments of Initiation apart from the Easter Vigil).

15. See Ibid., nos. 756 – 760 (2. Christian Initiation of Children).

ACKNOWLEDGMENTS

Excerpts from <u>Environment and Art in Catholic Worship</u> and <u>National Statutes for the Catechumenate</u> © 1978, 1988 United States Catholic Conference, Washington, D.C. All rights reserved. Used with permission.

Excerpts from <u>The Place of Worship</u> © 1994 Irish Episcopal Commission for Liturgy. All rights reserved. Used with permission.

Excerpts from the English translation of the <u>Book of Blessings</u> © 1988 International Committee on English in the Liturgy, Inc. All rights reserved. Used with permission.

The ancient baptismal fonts of North Africa and southern Europe provide us with valuable lessons for understanding fonts today. When baptizing in rivers and lakes was no longer feasible, early Christian churches designed fonts to serve their rites and in response to their fundamental questions about the meaning of baptism. Their answers — and even more so their questions — are invaluable to us today as we seek to renew the celebration of baptism by renewing architectural forms.

Some think that the large fonts being built in churches today are a modern innovation. In fact, they are modern applications of ancient lessons. This essay is for all who seek to understand the font of holy baptism—parishioners, building committee members, designers and architects.

T. Jerome Overbeck, PhD, a priest of the Society of Jesus, is university liturgist at Loyola University, Chicago.

LTP

LITURGY
TRAINING
PUBLICATIONS

ISBN 1-56854-091-4

90000

9 781568 540917

FONTS
$6.00